Love divine

Stefka Harp

Love divine
© Stefka Mladenova 2014, revised 2015

All rights reserved. No part of this publication may be reproduced, stored in a retrieval system, or transmitted in any form or by any means, electronic, mechanical, photocopying, recording or otherwise, without the prior written permission of the author.

National Library of Australia Cataloguing-in-Publication entry

Creator: Harp, Stefka, author.

Title: Love divine.

ISBN: 978-0-9923040-4-1

Subjects: Australian poetry

Published with the assistance of www.wordwrightediting.com.au

Images courtesy of clker.com.

www.stefkaharp.com

Contents

Acknowledgements v

Dedication vi

Introduction vii

Love hopes 1

Love wins them all 2

Love prospers 4

Love is kind 5

Love is the greatest 6

Love and delight in loving yourself 8

Love is patient 10

Love trusts 11

Love is victorious 12

Love is not easily angered 14

Love is glorious 16

Love endures 17

Love does not delight in evil 18

Love does not keep records of wrongs 20

Love perseveres 22

Love or envy 23

Love is not self-seeking 24

Love encourages 26

Love and peace 27
Love conquers 28
Love protects 29
Love does not fear 30
Love is not rude 32
Love respects 33
Love and grace upon yourself 34
Love is an eternal blessing 36
Love does not boast 38
Love does not envy 40
Love the Divine 42
Love never fails 44
Love glorifies 46
Love forgives 47
Love is not proud 48
Loving attitude 49
Love accepts us for who we are 50
About the author 52

Love divine

Acknowledgements

I wish to express my deep and sincere gratitude to my parents for teaching me the value of life — how to love and be happy as well as show kindness; and to my siblings, for being a part of my life.

My thanks, too, to the Australian Government for opening the door for me to migrate and become a permanent resident; to experience a different kind of life, culture and customs, which has been very enriching, enlightening and eye-opening. I am very grateful for the opportunity I have been given and guided to get to the point I am at.

Sincere gratitude to:

- my daughter for her patience and loving assistance in proofreading my work
- Alison Leader for her editing
- my publishing advisor for assistance given
- my niece Maria and my loyal friends who were willing to read my manuscripts and give constructive comments and feedback.

Dedication

Everything I write and have written so far is dedicated to my family and the divine within, which has guided me through life. At times my ignorance and oblivion to the facts revealed has led to strife and suffering. But these experiences have given me the much-needed fuel for my writings, and I hope they will help others. Life is like a jigsaw puzzle. Some things are meant to happen so that the pieces fit within that puzzle.

S.H.

Introduction

When we read anything on any topic, our brain takes time to filter and process the information we read, deciding what to let in and what to discard. What we choose to retain also depends on our individual life experience, beliefs and convictions about a particular topic.

It's a different story altogether when someone has had a shock. The brain doesn't have time to filter and process. The information surpasses all the barriers and goes directly in, etching deeply into the brain. That's why individuals who've had a shocking experience have flashbacks, nightmares and post-traumatic stress. It takes a long time to extinguish the deeply etched memory.

Stefka, an author of self-help books, has examined the difference between these experiences, and thought about ways to help her spiritual growth. She's written poems in a form of affirmations to help the healing process. These poems are very powerful and to the point. There is no time for processing the message, as it is absorbed immediately. She uses powerful, positive words that aim at shifting people's thoughts into positive territory within their psyche, which in turn brings joy and happiness — and with time, peace and harmony, uniting with the Divine within. When read, particularly before bedtime, the subconscious takes over, and after awhile a shift in the person's thoughts is noticed.

From personal experience, she is totally convinced it does work.

Stefka has often heard expressions such as: 'This is real', 'the real world', 'reality of life' and so on. What is real and reality? Well, what is real for one person could be something entirely different for someone else. Stefka has come to know that reality is the total sum of one's life experience. Reality is what we make it, and that's how diversity is created.

Over a lifetime, depending on the above factors, needs and wants, we create habits which are hard to extinguish. It's been said it takes twenty-one days to make a habit or break one. Stefka, being a person of integrity and wanting to know what's real and what's not, has been experimenting with creating habits and breaking them. There are no good or bad habits. It all depends on personal choice and preferences.

She had recent success with breaking a habit of drinking Turkish coffee. This drink is as black as night, strong, and thick as mud. Stefka had been drinking it for more than forty years. She knew it wasn't doing her any good, but kept drinking it anyway, because she felt she could not do without it.

One day, as she was just about to drink her morning coffee as usual, she said: 'This is poison my body can do without,' then went ahead and drank the coffee. You have noticed that she did not use words like: 'I shouldn't', 'I wouldn't', or any other negatives. Why? Because we like being free and unrestricted, and we take no notice of the negatives. The human brain does not like restrictions.

Years ago she knew someone who wanted to stop smoking. Every time she lit a cigarette she said: 'I don't like smoking.' The more she said the phrase, the

Love divine

stronger the craving became, and she was smoking more cigarettes a day then before. When Stefka made her aware of the way the brain responds to negative words, she developed another affirmation with no negatives, and it didn't take long for her to give up smoking. One day she took one puff and threw the cigarette away — and never went back to smoking.

Back to Stefka and her Turkish coffee. The next morning she said the same words as the day before and drank the coffee. She repeated the ritual every morning as she was drinking the freshly made coffee, lovingly sweetened with honey as always. As she was doing this, the taste of the coffee started to take on a different feel. It wasn't as delicious and pleasant anymore. It was the same coffee, out of the same jar — but it tasted horrible.

One morning when she took the first sip of the coffee, she felt like she had poison in her mouth. She spat it out, poured the rest down the drain, put the jar with the rest of the coffee in the bin, and hasn't looked back. There were no cravings for the coffee, ever. The brain was conditioned to think it was poison and reacted appropriately.

Even though she wasn't craving for the coffee, there was a feeling of missing something by not drinking the coffee. Then it dawned on her. After she drank the coffee she read her coffee cup — it was her daily horoscope. She realised that the cup-reading was her primary reason for drinking the coffee. She told herself that cup-reading was not her desire anymore. Not long after she was free from that habit as well.

The brain likes things that bring pleasure, which in turn pleases the soul. If it is pleasing to the brain and the soul, the person is compelled to do it. The urge is strong and irresistible. But if you know how to break

Stefka Harp

the pattern by understanding how the mind works, and with persistent repetition of positive affirmations, eventually there would be success.

Stefka Harp

Disclaimer: The author is expressing beliefs and views based on her life experience. There is no intention to offend anyone who has contrary views. The poems are fun to read and in the process can bring a positive and loving attitude.

Love divine

Like the sun in the sky,
Outshine and stand high.
Valse the tune in the hope of
Everlasting peace and truth.

Hope and faith, hand in hand,
Onward marching by,
Princely all the way,
Endlessly, until the day
Serenity, love and joy are on the way.

Stefka Harp

Live in spirit, love like a child,
Only things that come to mind.
Vibrant love is here to stay,
Ever more loving thoughts to convey,

Well and truly to win the day,
In its entirety, come what may.
None other but the Divine,
Saintly, will guide you love to find.

Love divine

Timeless faith and hope,
Harmoniously with love let you cope.
Else, faith and hope would come to a halt
Meanwhile, if love is not beheld.

Approach life with love,
Lady luck will fit like a glove,
Last of all, be loyal to yourself and
                          pure as a dove.

Love is followed by faith and hope,
Of course lady luck no doubt,
Visible, it might not seem so,
Even when you're quite sure.

Prosperity is not always about money,
Revelation you might find funny,
Overflow of love and loving thoughts, is a
Small step – a big leap of sorts.
Positive attitude is a wealth,
Essential to bring good health. If you
Radiate love, health and happiness,
Sure enough abundance will manifest.

Love is loyalty to yourself.
Opulence forever so,
Vivacious and always on the go,
Entirely devoted to the core.

Inspiring selflessness to the world,
Serenity for all.

Kindness when you know
It is when happiness flows,
Necessary to find the Divine,
Do not ever resign from being kind.

Stefka Harp

Love is dynamic forever more,
Oceans of blessings on the way galore,
Very real and always on the go,
Endless happiness and joy to the fore.

Insofar as you guard your thoughts,
Sure enough they become words.

Then deeds follow in all fairness,
Hence loving thoughts create greatness,
Everlasting peace and wellness.

Love divine

Graciously gallop along the path of love,
Rediscover the power of it all,
Entirely immerse yourself to the core,
Allow love and loving thoughts
To guide and inspire words.
Endear and persevere forever more,
Suffice to say wisdom gained galore,
Trust the higher love you adore.

Let's say divine light comes within,
Overnight while sleeping,
Vitality bestowed upon yourself in delight
Every day and night.

Always!
No one else, but the
Divine will do the rest.

Dance and prance forever so,
Eagerly the way you know,
Life is yours to enjoy,
Insist on loving thoughts to deploy.
Generate courage at your best,
Hard and fast with your request,
Today is the time for conquest.

Infinite mind will do the rest,
Now and forever to be blessed.

Love divine

Leaning to love yourself is not a breeze,
Off you go and do the quiz,
Validate what you know.
Indefinitely, be sure
Never to turn the sting within,
Grace and love only, and no quitting.

Yes, delight in loving yourself,
Openly and of free will,
Utmost sincerity, and be thrilled,
Ready to restore self-esteem.
Selection of thoughts and words in favour of
Endless gratitude to treasure,
Life is to be enjoyed, do not measure,
Forgiveness will bring great pleasure.

Listen to your heart,
Open your mind,
View the world,
Eagerly with love and care.

It is divinely so,
Slow down and look around.

Patience is a virtue, it
Allows you to shine and grow.
Thankfully ever so, more
Immediately to restore
Everlasting peace you adore.
Necessary it is to flow
Throughout life, happiness galore.

Love divine

Love, love and more love,
Only love will win glory,
Very much so for you to grow,
Eternally and forever so.

Tranquility will be upon yourself,
Ready to discover yourself, upon
Unifying with the Divine.
Speak the truth and truth be known,
Trust and integrity are shown.
Somehow, without trust, love wouldn't thrive.

Live life as one with the Divine,
Only way to be a winner every time.
Visualise a success, and
Expect to be blessed.

Important it is to be precise,
Sound enough advice.

Love divine

Voice your wants and needs,
Innermost good deeds,
Clarify every detail,
Trust in God, never be in denial.
Repetition is the score,
Instantly you will go to explore
Opportunity to learn and grow,
Unfolding love in your core,
Safeguarding your victory for sure.

Love is patient, love is kind,
Out goes your loving mind,
Vigorously sending blessings,
Endless well wishes expressing.

In the meantime, love is to cherish,
Surrender to it or perish.

Neither in anger make decisions, nor
Overwhelm yourself with precisions,
Take your time, but not for long,

Else procrastination will invite itself in,
Anger might flair, but do not dwell.
Sit in silence and become aware,
Imminently to declare,
Love always aims to repair.
Yippee! There goes dazzling glare.

Love divine

Another day goes by,
None other but the Divine
Gracefully will guide and protect
Eternally, until the anger dissipates.
Radiance and peace is gained,
Endless happiness is attained,
Devotion to love is retained.

Let love into your life,
Outshine, but not with pride.
Venture into it to find,
Emerge into a divine child.

Infinitely forever more,
Serenity to find and undergo

Graceful transformation with time,
Love a plenty, which is not a crime,
Opportunity to explore with a smile,
Rest assured, it will be a trial.
Important it is to know
One must do the chore
Unfailing, for the love to flow,
Sufficient to make yourself glow.

Love divine

Life is trial and error,
Obvious as can be,
Vow to give nothing but love,
Endless blessings and well wishing.

Endurance is a virtue, it
Never gives up or resigns.
Diligently it goes on,
Undeniably moving forward,
Rest assured, to get you there.
Even if you fail,
Song and praise for the wisdom gained.

Love illuminates the way,
Occasion to celebrate and be gay,
Vigorously as you can, and say,
Everlasting love is here to stay.

Dedicate yourself to be kind,
Overall impression on your mind, for
Evermore without a fear,
Stand high and make it clear.

Now you are talking, my dear.
Over and above be true and sincere,
The Divine is always there to hear.

Designate time for prayer, for
Evermore to prepare,
Loving thoughts to deploy,
Insistent evil feelings to destroy.
Generate strength and be bold,
Honour and dignity to uphold,
Truth is never to withhold.

Love divine

Inspire the mind,
New ways of thinking to find, for

Ever to thrive.
Vengeance and evil leave behind,
Innocence let come to the fore,
Life infused with love to flow.

Love makes you feel alive,
Only way everyone can thrive,
Victory in your life,
Everlasting peaceful mind.

Diverge from love and truth,
Ouch! It will hurt and bite.
Engage in something constructive,
Somehow life turns out to be delightful.

No one ever benefited,
Or has been overjoyed,
To have a tendency ever so, in

Keeping records of wrongs.
Endlessly the pain prolongs,
Each time hostility grows,
Pride and ego in defence gnaw.

Love divine

Rejuvenate your good will and delight,
Everything is going to be alright.
Conquer the urge to be picky
Onward only, and don't be tricky.
Rejoice and be happy.
Dwell in the belief of being blessed,
Sensible thing to do at best.

Off you go, dismantle the list,
Forgiveness will do the rest.

Wrong everyone in life has done,
Reference to the wrong is like pointing a gun.
Only express feelings when the wrong is done,
Never to refer to it is number one.
Grasp the wisdom of not keeping records,
Start loving and live life instead.

Loving thoughts on your mind is
One of many positive signs,
Verify what you want,
Evoke passion for as long.

Patience will be upon yourself,
Energising to carry on.
Right the wrong and apologise,
Sensible thing to recognise,
Endlessly and forever more,
Various options to explore,
Exactly how to get to the core.
Request obstacles to be gone,
Everlasting peace restored,
Smile and persevere, joy will follow for sure.

Love divine

Love is in abundance and very sound,
Only if you choose to look around.
Visualise sending love out there,
Endless saturations everywhere.

Or if you choose envy,
Repercussions you are sure to gain.

Eerie, it will not seem so,
None-the-less the suffering will flow,
Vanity will dominate, hurting will bestow,
Yet for another day, endlessly on the go.

Love is glorious and not a chore.
Only you could come to that door,
Valuable lesson to acquire,
Elevate the soul and admire.

Indeed, needy people all around,
Situations to do something about,

Neither fear nor shy away,
Opportunity to say
Tender words of praise.

Love divine

Seize the moment and be kind,
Enjoy giving some of your time,
Let the Divine within guide,
Feel joy and have a peaceful mind.

Sheer pleasure to have trials,
Expected to do the miles,
Elevate your spirit and give smiles.
Kick the habit of self-seeking,
Indulge in more giving.
Now and forever as you would,
Gracefully, yet humbly, as you should.

Leave no stone unturned,
Openly and honestly,
Vastly high and low,
Elevate your soul.

Enjoy life as it stands,
None-the-less, make amends.
Complete all the chores,
Obligation to the cause.
Unburden and spread your wings,
Rejoice flying in the winds.
Approach matters with love and care,
Generously if you dare,
Every step of the stairs,
Suddenly you are there.

Love divine

Love is delightfully calm,
Overjoyed with goodness of yourself,
Vigorously on the go,
Excellent to the core.

Always praise and pray,
Never turn away,
Demand love and peace every day.

Precious love means you don't stray,
Ever so peacefully on your way.
Always treasure and adore,
Calmness upon yourself in accord,
Earnest well-wishing to the world.

Long to give unconditional love,
Often and pure as a dove.
Vow to be gentle and kind,
Endlessly to be on your mind.

Choose love instead and smile,
Only way to spend the time,
Necessary if you want to be healthy,
Quietly, you will start feeling wealthy.
Unreal it might seem so,
Engage in the game and do the score,
Repetition of the same and more,
Sense happiness on your way galore.

Love divine

Life is not always predictable,
One way only for ever more,
Very real and unavoidable,
Even when you are not aware.

Persist and make no question,
Rejoice in the knowledge, and
Obey the wisdom within.
Trust and love go so far,
Embrace them with all your heart.
Confidence is on the way, and more,
Tender loving care to bestow,
Safety and protection for sure.

Stefka Harp

Love is sincere and oh so dear,
Off you go and renounce the fear,
Victory is sweet and near,
Evidently it is so clear.

Dwell on love in delight,
Often as you like,
Embrace it with all your might,
Soothe the mind and have a good night.

Love divine

Nurture the seed of love and hope,
Overjoyed knowing you can do the work,
Take the time to do the walk.

Fascinate yourself with blessings,
Excellent way for progressing,
Acknowledge the inception of the fear,
Request love and cheer, and let the fear
                               disappear.

Love is gentle all the time,
Onward forever marching by,
Vigorous is love,
Ever so pure like a dove,

In so far as all is good,
Sing a song and be merry.

Never be unkind or rude,
Only beam with love and joy,
To enable yourself to be kind.

Rest assured when something is said,
Undeniably speaks more about yourself,
Desire to say something good,
Else, if you can't, say nothing at all.

Love divine

Love is like so,
Omnipotent and on the go,
Vast and serene always galore,
Extremely humble forever more.

Respect is a remarkable gesture though,
Excellent virtue, amazingly so,
Slow down, praise and bless the way you know.
Priority is to show respect to yourself and all,
Ever more so, do not neglect the world.
Compassion you would come to find,
Tremendous union with the Divine,
Sing and dance, rain or shine.

Love heals and restores,
Overnight bestows,
Vitality upon yourself,
Eternal peace to dwell.

Always on the go,
Non-stop to explore,
Delightfully to the core.

Grant yourself the honour of the day,
Rediscover the inner strength as you may,
Allow spirituality to grow,
Cherish the progress that you know,
Emerge victorious and glow.

Love divine

Undergone many trials,
Peace-loving child,
Out you go, and be kind,
Now is the time for love and grace to find.

You are unique,
One and only, not a freak,
Unlikely to play at mystique,
Rather, love divine you would seek.
Spring up and leave worries behind,
Express loving thoughts and shine,
Last but not least, my dear friend, send
Forgiveness to the world, ever so grand.

Love forever and smile,
Only way to find a
Vast and vigorous life,
Eternal peace to thrive.

Invoke loving thoughts within,
Smile more often on greeting.

Adress others with respect,
No more, no less.

Eminently, though,
True loving thoughts project more,
Endeavour to make a habit, for sure.
Ray of hope soon will be prancing,
Now and then to make the soul dancing,
Amazing! What a blessing from herein,
Lively spirit to shine within.

Love divine

Beaming with radiance upon the world,
Life immersed in love is like gold.
Eternal spirit will come upon you and glow,
Sound advice is to let it grow,
Sensible thing to do. So
Inner peace and joy,
Nurtured with love instead of worry,
Gracefully will thrive and glory.

Life, in a manner of speaking, can be simple,
Only if you desire it so.
Veneration is the way to go,
Either for yourself or the world.

Dare to be humble,
Onward marching by,
Ever-so-kind,
Sensible attitude to find.

Neither boast nor be proud,
Overly knowing how,
Tell the truth as it is.

Before anybody finds out,
Overall emblazon the story,
Almost making others doubt.
Secretly they will be laughing
To hear someone bragging.

Love is all around,
One-and-only makes the world go round,
Very real and ever-so present,
Ensuring life is quite pleasant.

Desire to inspire,
Only way to go,
Eminently so,
Sensible thing to acquire.

Love divine

Never plant the seed of envy, it
Overflows and spills out, and
Truth is perverted and undermined.

Enemies plenty for sure,
None of them wants to know the
Validity of the tittle-tattle,
Yet one continues to rattle-prattle.

Lordly walk the path of your destiny,
Overjoyed in knowing the
Vigorous life you have to thrill,
Ever so to live and destiny fulfil.

Trust yourself and shine,
Heavenly, one day at a time, and
Embrace the Divine.

Love divine

Discover the peace within,
Impress loving thoughts on greeting,
Very real they are, so send them out,
Instantly without doubt,
Necessary for you to continue to pray,
Endless loving thoughts to convey.

Love goes on, with all the wisdom,
Over and above aim for love in God's kingdom.
Validate the Divine within,
Earnest wish for an angel to be greeting.

Now, throw old habits to the winds,
Elevate your soul and grow wings,
Vanquish your fears and do not snooze,
Else if you do, you might lose,
Remedy the ego and do not let it bruise.

Love divine

Forgiveness is love, you would agree,
Another way to be free,
In part with pain, to a degree.
Last but not least, take a vow,
Swallow your pride and let love guide.

Learn the wisdom of love,
Overflowing, it will fit like a glove.
Visualise you love the rose in the garden,
Energy will flow, encouraging you to be ardent.

Gorgeous garnish for the spirit,
Love doesn't know how to limit,
Obligation to love is not a gimmick.
Romance the thought of loving,
Indeed, everything that crawls around.
Forgive if you must and persist,
Infinitely, and do not dismiss,
Envisage it's here and do not sway,
Serenity and glory will be on the way.

Love divine

Loving thoughts on your mind,
Only way to spend time,
Vast and vigorous it is so,
Enough to hug the world and more.

Ferocious is your desire,
Openly to forgive and admire,
Radiance about to transpire,
Generous nature to acquire.
Ideal it is to forgive every day,
Vanquish the evil and do not stray.
Effuse your mind with loving thoughts,
Send them out, indeed, with loving words.

Love is humble and always on the go,
Occasional opportunity to explore,
Vengeance never on your mind,
Eagerness to be kind is a good sign.

Insist on being humble forever more,
Seek truth and love galore.

Nobody benefits as far as one knows,
Of being proud, and spirituality grows,
Topsy-turvy in one's life to be precise.

Pave the way for harmonious life to last,
Request guidance if you must.
On the lookout with a quest,
Urging proud gesture to be put to rest,
Do away with it, with a loving request.

Life is a learning process,
Onward marching by,
Various thoughts on your mind.
Influencing attitudes immensely so,
Never intentionally to harm or hurt, only
Glimmer of hope to alert.

Amazingly, slowly but surely,
Transformation should follow for sure,
Thoughts and words to inspire,
Invoking righteousness to desire.
Time has come to right the wrong,
Unconditional love to come to the fore,
Dreams are made forever more,
Enfolding life tremendously so.

Living a life to thrill, as
Often as I feel,
Voraciously! I let it be,
Everyone to know and see.

Address others I do, with respect,
Choice of loving thoughts I incorporate, and
Concentrate on acceptance.
End result is connection,
Peaceful resolution and protection
Throughout the journey of my life,
Sufficient to sustain my spiritual drive.

Unconditional love I send out,
Sacred heart I have, without doubt.

Love divine

Faithfully from now on I would go
On and only spiritually grow,
Ready holiness to know.

Well and truly I smile,
Hoping to have a hassle-free time
Once in a while.

Warm gratitude to the Divine,
Eager for fears to be left behind.

Accepting others and ourselves for who we are,
Ready for joyful rapture,
Endless happiness to capture.

About the author

Stefka was born during World War II in a small village tucked away in the foothills of a big mountain in Eastern Macedonia.

Her family, like others in the village, gained their food from the land. It was a self-sufficient household. This lifestyle built much confidence in her and her siblings.

She migrated to Australia in 1972, where she still resides. She finished her degree, and a diploma in counselling, and gained jobs in the welfare sector.

The last seven years before retirement were spent in the DV sector. While working with people she noticed the power of thought in relation to destiny. She believes that when people change their thinking and implement positive and loving thoughts, life changes for better. Prayer, forgiveness, hope and faith go hand in hand with a positive attitude.

Academic achievements

Diploma of Community Services Management

    Southbank Institute of TAFE 2006

Diploma in Counselling

    Australian Institute of Counsellors 1993–1994

Bachelor of Arts Degree (Major Psychology)

    University of Queensland 1989

Economics, book keeping & accounting

    Business Studies College (Macedonia)

www.ingramcontent.com/pod-product-compliance
Lightning Source LLC
Chambersburg PA
CBHW061250040426
42444CB00010B/2334